PENNY STOCKS

**Understanding, Investing and Trading Penny Stocks
for Beginners
A Guide On How To Make Money On The Stock Market
the Cheap Way**

Descrierea CIP a Bibliotecii Naţionale a României
CARTER, MATTHEW G.
   Penny Stocks. Understanding, Investing and Trading Penny
Stocks for Beginners. A Guide On How To Make Money On
The Stock Market the Cheap Way / Matthew G. Carter. –
Bucuresti: My Ebook, 2018
   ISBN 978-606-983-590-6

PENNY STOCKS

Understanding, Investing and Trading Penny Stocks for Beginners

A Guide On How To Make Money On The Stock Market the Cheap Way

INTRODUCTION

I want to thank you and congratulate you for downloading the book, *"Penny Stocks: Understanding, Investing and Trading Penny Stocks for Beginners: A Guide on How to Make Money on the Stock Market the Cheap Way"*.

This book has actionable information on how to invest in penny stocks, trade penny stocks and make money in the process.

Investing in stocks is undoubtedly one of the best investment vehicles the world over. And it is not just the high value stocks that cost tens, hundreds or even thousands of dollars per share; even if you invest in stocks that cost less than $10 or even less than $5 per share, you stand a good chance to make a lot of money in the process, especially in capital gains. If you cannot afford to spare 10s, 100s or even 1000s of dollars per share, perhaps penny stocks are the way to go. Even if you are completely new to stocks trading and penny stocks in particular, you can learn everything there is to learn about these and succeed at it. There is just so much money to be made trading in penny stocks and this book will show you exactly what you need to do.

If you are one of those people who think that you have to be a trading prodigy to invest in penny stocks then you are very wrong. Penny stocks, just like any other stocks and securities, require you to be well informed, disciplined and have good strategies while participating in order to succeed – and this is what this guide is meant for. It will give you sufficient knowledge that you will require to get started as a penny stock trader inclusive of how to trade, calculating your profits, avoiding penny stocks hazards and much more!

This is where your penny stock success journey begins.

Thanks again for downloading this book. I hope you enjoy it!

This document is geared towards providing exact and reliable information in regards to the topic and issue covered. The publication is sold with the idea that the publisher is not required to render accounting, officially permitted, or otherwise, qualified services. If advice is necessary, legal or professional, a practiced individual in the profession should be ordered.

– From a Declaration of Principles which was accepted and approved equally by a Committee of the American Bar Association and a Committee of Publishers and Associations.

In no way is it legal to reproduce, duplicate, or transmit any part of this document in either electronic means or in printed format. Recording of this publication is strictly prohibited and any storage of this document is not allowed unless with written permission from the publisher. All rights reserved.

The information provided herein is stated to be truthful and consistent, in that any liability, in terms of inattention or otherwise, by any usage or abuse of any policies, processes, or directions contained within is the solitary and utter responsibility of the recipient reader. Under no circumstances will any legal responsibility or blame be held against the publisher for any reparation, damages, or monetary loss due to the information herein, either directly or indirectly.

TABLE OF CONTENTS

Penny Stocks: A Comprehensive Background

Penny Stock: What Is It?

In simple terms, a penny stock is basically a low priced stock that is trading under $5. They are common stocks owned and made available by small public companies. The low price of penny stock shares allows an investor to hold many shares (typically thousands) at the same time for a small amount of invested capital. This explains why penny stocks are so appealing and offer competitive advantage to small and medium sized investors.

Most people make money off penny stocks by benefiting from the capital gains i.e. the appreciation of price of shares, as most penny stocks don't pay dividends.

As amazing as this sounds, this profit model makes penny stocks also highly risky – as much as they offer high returns. This is because of one major reason – they are more prone to scams. Some of the common scams you should look out for are such as:

1: Pump and Dump Schemes

This is where promoters attract interest for an unknown or a scarcely known stock. Potential clueless investors buy up the shares which in turn pump up the share price. Once the stock is nicely inflated up to a certain price, the scammers dump the stocks for a huge profit, which leaves the investors stranded. These schemes are usually popularized through free penny stock newsletters so if you get your hands on one of those, check them out carefully before making a move.

2: Reverse merger

There comes a time where a private company merges with a public company to make themselves public without going through the whole traditional process. This gives the private company an opportunity to falsify its earnings and in turn raise its stock prices – which they usually offer in penny stocks. While some of the mergers are legit, it is important to review the history of the business undergoing the reverse merger.

3: The Guru Scam

If you have been researching on investing in penny stocks, then I'm pretty sure you have come across a 'penny stock guru' ad. These are false ads which show you how penny stock expert got rich by using a 'special' technique (they even go as far as showing you pictures of their fancy cars, mansions and boats). The guru then promises to make you as rich by sharing with you this 'special' technique for just a one-time fee. You will pay the fee and end up with a not so special technique that's a rip off from the internet.

The truth is, even if the guru got rich from penny stocks, one size doesn't fit all when it comes to riches, and especially not when it comes to the stock market.

4: Short and Distort Schemes

This is the reverse of pump and dump where investors short sell to make a profit. Shorting is where an investor borrows shares and sells them in the open market at a really high price with the aim of causing a fall in the company's stock so that he can buy the sold shares at a lower price. The investor then returns the borrowed shares to the lender and lands a profit.

So penny stock swindlers short sell a stock then make sure the stock falls through spreading false and harmful rumors about that company. The short sellers end up making money while you end up holding a losing stock.

5: Offshore Scams

Companies that operate outside of the country, e.g. in the United States, are not required to register their shares with the U.S. Securities Exchange Commission when selling to offshore investors. Penny stock scammers seize this opportunity. They purchase unregistered and inexpensive shares from companies at an offshore location then sell to investors in the U.S. at a higher price. The instreaming of the unregistered shares lead to a drop in the company's stock price. The scammers end up with huge profits while you as an investor is left with little, if any, to pocket.

So what should you do about the penny stock scams; how do you avoid them? Let's discuss that:

How to Avoid Penny Stock Scams

Without a doubt, the penny stock world is full of frauds, but as an investor, you should not be intimidated by that – every endeavor has its risks and scams exist everywhere. You simply need to know how to avoid scams and you'll be good. Here are some ideas on how to make that happen:

1. Spot the difference between research and promotion.

Promoters usually hire newsletter writers to come up with luring reports on their stocks. The writers compose something persuasive in relation to investing in fake penny stocks comprising of projections and sometimes intentional distortions to make their promotional creations seem like real research reports.

However, you as the investor, you need to distinguish between the real and the fake. One sure way is by reading the 'disclosures' section at the end. If it shows that the writer is directly compensated for the report (normally through a combination of stock and cash) by the company they are promoting, then that would essentially make it a mere advertisement and not an actual research report.

2. Check the financials of the company.

Generally, penny stocks don't dispense thorough financial info but you should take a step and check the financial statements that the company releases. Analyze the balance sheet to see if the company has a huge amount of debt or liabilities in arrears plus the net cash at hand. Make sure to also check the income statement and if it shows a huge growth in revenues currently, then that's a good sign.

3. Check the credibility of the company's management.

The quality of the management highly influences the success of a company. Though you don't expect to find a Bill Gates running a penny stock company, do research on the company's directors and executives. Find out their strategies, if they have had any significant failures, success, legal issues etc.

4. Check the quality of disclosure.

Companies with a greater level of corporate transparency are better to invest in – they have nothing to hide. Try and avoid companies that provide limited or no information.

5. Check if the business plan is achievable

You should evaluate whether the plan of the company you are interested in buying stocks is achievable and also if it indeed has the professed asset base.

With what we've learned so far in mind, let's now move on to discussing how and where to trade penny stocks.

Where And How To Trade Penny Stocks

When it comes to where to trade penny stocks, there are those stock markets that are great for trading and those that should be avoided, as they are dangerous to investors. You should, therefore, choose your market wisely – don't worry, I will help. Some of the markets that penny stocks trade are:

NASDAQ SmallCap Market

NASDAQ

(National Association

of Securities Dealers Automated Quotations)

SmallCap is literally the best and safest market to trade penny stocks. The companies listed here have systematic reporting conditions that must be followed for them to maintain their listing. This will enable you to have access to the company's ongoing results and end of financial year reports.

Normally, the penny shares listed here go for a dollar and up. If by any chance a company listed on NASDAQ SmallCap starts trading for less than a dollar, the exchange boosts their stock which forces them to move to OTC BB (which I'll explain below).

The visibility that comes with trading penny shares on NASDAQ SmallCap market (as most news services and financial quote cover these shares) improves investor participation and trading volume.

These shares usually have 4 letter ticker symbols (abbreviations to uniquely identify shares traded publicly) such as DRAX, IDEV and PVAT.

OTC-BB (Over-The-Counter Bulletin Board)

The OTC-BB is owned and operated by NASDAQ so it is also very legit. This is a regulated quotation service which displays last sale prices, real time quotes and volume info in OTC equity securities.

This OTC BB equity security is basically any equity that isn't listed or traded on a national security exchange or NASDAQ. In short, it is a system that creates some systematization and answerability for those stocks that 'don't have a home'. Some of the few characteristics of OTC BB are:

- It provides access to more than 3600 securities.
- It displays prior day trading activity and indication of interest.
- It electronically transmits real time quote, volume information and price.
- It involves more than 330 participating markets.

AMEX

Just like the NASDAQ SmallCap, the AMEX (The American Stock Exchange) is a great market for penny stocks. The shares here might have less volume than those on NASDAQ SmallCap but the companies are still required to place their reports with the exchange and are followed by a lot of quote and news services – so you will still enjoy the same benefits as SmallCap.

Pink Sheets Penny Stocks

These should be avoided at all costs. These are stocks that trade with no regulation or reporting requirements and also have no responsibility to you the investor. They are so hard to buy and sell since their trading activity is really low and irregular.

Pink sheets penny stocks have fewer rules and fewer listing requirements – if this doesn't sound like trouble to you, I don't know what does.

Penny Stocks Straight from Companies

In some cases, it is possible to buy shares directly from the company of interest. The reason people do this, mostly, is to avoid paying brokerage commission. It may also be an easier way to get stock from a more secluded company instead of trading for them over the counter.

As much as this is slightly better than over the counter stocks, there are a few predicaments when it comes to buying directly. For starters, you have no assurance that you will get a fair valuation in relation to the prevailing market prices – actually in most cases the amount is always higher than what you would have paid on an exchange. Also, the trading volumes may be non-existent and it may be hard to sell (as easy as it is to buy). The point here is, you will have no way of knowing so avoid this at all costs – if you have no knowledge of the company or don't know the management directly.

Penny Stocks over the Phone

In this case, NEVER accept any offer to purchase penny stocks (or any other stocks for that matter) over an unsolicited call, fax or even email.

The companies here are promoted zealously and for most of them, they are non-existent, run poorly vacant nothings. It is close to impossible to resell these equities. These 'promoters' will pressure you with a specific time frame and demand immediate action from you with no data or information about the company (fake if any).

If you get a call and it is something like this, just hand up the phone, don't say a thing. If you get your hands on the movie 'Boiler Room', be sure to watch it. It will drive this point home.

Canadian Markets

Both TSK (The Toronto Stock Exchange) and TSX-V (Toronto Venture Exchange) list penny stock shares with some going for as low as just a couple of cents. Get yourself a broker who allows over the border trades.

Canadian penny stocks trade so inexpensively priced because they are much smaller in size and not because they are highly speculative and extremely long shots. There are literally thousands of legit Canadian penny stocks companies to choose from.

-Before You Begin Trading...

1: Involve yourself in some paper trading in penny stocks

Paper trading, also known as virtual stock trading, is a simulated trading process where investors practice trading without paying out any real money. This is an easy and realistic way of learning the basics of penny stock trading and you don't risk even a penny.

2: Document your objectives

Take my word for it; if you really don't know where you are headed, then you will land on any path as an investor. This is very risky especially when it comes to penny stocks – as you can even be easily lured by the unsolicited penny callers.

Therefore, write down your penny stock objectives such as which stocks you want to invest in, the markets you will trade on, the price ranges that you are interested in, the industry group you prefer – whether tech, biotech, transportation etc. and any other details you deem important.

3: Get a broker, if you don't have one

Use the money you intend to invest with to open an account. There are basically 2 types of brokers that you could decide on:

- A discount broker

This is the ideal kind of broker for penny stocks. You can simply open an online trading account where you will be able to monitor and view all your trades, get quotes and info for those penny stocks you are interested in and also access your history of transactions.

These are also cheaper as they usually allow trades for a small fee such as just $5.

- A full service broker

These brokers deal one on one with a client and are best suited for investors with a large portfolio. Their commissions are pretty high (several hundred dollars) for a trade that you could have made for only about $15 through a discount broker.

-Trading Penny Stocks

Trading penny stocks is rather easy and not different from when you are dealing with other equities. It is as simple as going online to your broker and clicking 'buy these, sell those', and that's it. But you need to have a good stock broker for this. For a deeper understanding of trading penny stocks:

Let's assume that you are interested in shares of XYZ Corporation and the penny stock ticker symbol is XYZA.

You want to put in about $500 and their stock last traded at 45 cents. You make the choice of buying thinking that the price will upsurge. You log in to your brokerage account and put in that you want to buy 1000 shares of XYZA and click submit. There you go, you just bought penny stocks.

Your account will reflect 1000 shares of your penny stocks XYZA of XYZ and if the price was still 45 cents during purchase then $450 will be deducted from the cash in your account for the purchase plus a couple of dollars for the commission (normally $15).

After a few months, let's say the price of XYZA goes up to 75 cents. You visit the portal and submit a trade via your broker to sell 1000 of your shares of XYZA. $750 are deposited to your account (less commission). This means that you made $300 worth of profit and now you've pocketed $750 to buy any other penny stocks you fancy.

Cancelling or Changing Open Trade Orders

Sometimes you might make an open order but then change your mind and decide to cancel it. It is simple to do as you just need to contact your broker but you will still be responsible for any prior fills. This means that in case 500 shares have been traded from your account before your cancellation then this part of the transaction cannot be reversed. Changing order is easy but try and not delay once you decide to make the change as prior fills cannot be changed.

In the case of changing the volume of your penny stocks (either buying or selling) you will have to place a new order for the additional number of shares. Be aware of the extra commission you will have to pay for the additional orders.

N.B. remember that penny stocks move with greater volatility than other investments so you have to stay on top of them.

Let's now discuss some strategies you should follow to increase your odds of success while trading penny stocks.

Strategies to Adhere To For Successful Trading In Penny Stocks

As easy as buying and selling penny stocks sounds, there are a number of strategies you need to apply to make sure your buying and selling is not in vain – trust me, it's not just as simple as buying and selling. If you don't know when to sell, buy or generally what to focus on, then your trading might not be as smooth. So which strategies should you keep in mind? Let's discuss that in detail:

First, NEVER listen to company management

In the world of trading penny stocks, don't make the mistake of listening to what companies whisper to you. It's close to impossible to trust anybody as the companies are just in the quest of raising money and keeping their business afloat.

Trust your own research on the company you buy shares from and the companies you are interested in buying stock from.

Sell quickly and don't sell short

An enticing quality of penny stocks is that it is possible to make around 20% to 30% returns in just a couple of days. If you happen to make that kind of profit with your penny stock then take it and sell right away.

26

Sadly, many investors get a bit ravenous and aim for 1000% profits. If you take into consideration that the penny stock you are holding might be in the process of getting pumped up, then you might want to go for what you get before you get nothing.

You should also avoid selling short when it comes to selling penny stocks – as attractive as selling short seems. Penny stocks are really volatile and if you find yourself on the losing end, you might end up losing 50% of your money or even more. It might also be difficult to find penny stock shares to sell shot.

Stick to penny stocks with a high volume

Focus on stocks that trade not less than 100, 000 shares in a day. Why is this important? Well, trading stocks with a low volume could mean getting stuck in the same position with your shares and also difficulty in finding a buyer. Make sure you know the dollar volume and the number of shares being traded.

You should also make a point of buying shares that go for more than 50 cents per share. Stocks priced for less than 50 cents (or trade less than 100, 000 shares a day) are considered to not be liquid enough to trade.

Check the earnings breakout

When buying, look for stocks that have had an earning breakout in their history. If you look well (deep research), these shares are easy to find and when you find them, consider your investment less risky.

Evaluate your position sizing

Your position sizing is the amount of money, stock or commodity that you chose to trade in a particulate transaction. Usually, when you feel too sure about a trade, you will end up trading big, and when you are not so sure about a trade, you will trade small – it is human nature. But you have to resist this norm and go for optimal trading – be somewhere in the middle. Think of if; you went big on a sure trade (say bought tons of shares from a company) and things take a turn for the unexpected – it would be detrimental for you.

Don't be random too. Know your position sizing before you trade.

The other thing you ought to be fully aware of is how to pick the right shares to trade and calculate your profits.

Tips for Picking a Winning Stock and Calculating Your Profits

In order for you to pick a winning penny stock, you will need both fundamental and technical analysis. Just because a particular stock seems attractive doesn't really mean that it is – you have to look at it at all angles.

Technical Analysis

This is generally the evaluation of your stock through studying any generated statistics regarding market activity such as volume and market price.

Price to Earnings (P/E)

This is probably the first thing you should look at. It simply shows what the company is trading at in respect to its per share earnings. Mostly, investors won't buy stock if this ratio goes above a certain level, such as 15 times.

The problem here is that the earnings can be easily manipulated and can include a number of special charges and/or write downs. On the other hand, a stock with a P/E of 5 times might be considered 'cheap' but you come to find out that there were one time earnings gains that might not likely be repeated.

A stock with a P/E of about 35 might seem expensive but you can find out that it had a large write down which messed up earnings in just a particular year.

The solution here is to obviously look at the P/E ratios of the stock but also look at what is behind those numbers.

Calculating Price to Earnings:

P/E ratio = price per share ÷ earnings per share (EPS)

The earnings per share (EPS) is calculated as:

EPS = earnings ÷ total shares outstanding

Price to Cash Flow

This is considerably a better and all rounded metric compared to the P/E ratio. This is because cash flow cannot be manipulated like earnings and for those dividend investors, the cash flow reflect whether the company can continue to pay dividends. The price to cash flow is the ratio of the stock's price to its cash flow per share.

Calculating price to cash flow

Price to cash flow= share price ÷ cash flow per share

Price/Earnings Momentum

This technique involves checking the momentum of price to earnings to identify a positive change. In this case, you check whether the companies are beating their earnings estimates with comparable price movements (ideally rising stock prices) and increases in the trading volume.

There is only one problem with this strategy, high momentum stocks are usually really expensive and once their momentum fades, the stock suffers miserably. This method is usually a good strategy though, especially when you are looking for new stock ideas.

Price to Book
This involves checking book value or accounting value and then comparing it to the current price of the stock. Sometimes you can buy a stock for much less than its real value using this technique.

It is quite a good technique but the major problem with it is that you have no way of making sure that the book value is real. For instance, mining and energy companies are taking huge write downs on assets which of course lower the book value. Other than that, the method is still considered key.

Fundamental Analysis

This involves generally analyzing everything from the management of companies to the overall economy and industry of the company.

When choosing the perfect stock, first make sure that the company you intend to buy stocks from is something you can understand to avoid unnecessary confusions. For instance, if you decide to buys shares in a tech company yet you don't understand anything, then you probably won't understand some expenses and revenues in their financial statements. Opt for easy to understand companies' stocks or companies you are familiar too – in terms of knowledge.

Second, check the long terms prospects of the company you want to buy penny stocks from. Does the company seem like it will be around decades from now? Do they have enough capital to last them a while? Dig deep into your mind.

Thirdly (this is more subjective), ensure that the company you are interested in has a competent and honest management. You don't want to put yourself through the torture of having sleepless nights since you can't trust the management of the company that you will be a partial owner of. You don't need to do a full on background check on the whole management team. Other investors or employees could give you a general idea of how the management is – or you could ask for a one on one with them and deduct your conclusion then.

Calculating Stock Profits

To calculate your stock profits:

Start by calculating the amount of money you paid to buy the penny stocks.

Multiply the share price (how much you paid for each share) by the number of the total shares that you bought – most online brokers do this for you so go ahead and check before taking out your calculator.

If you purchased some of your shares at different prices and times, do each calculation separately and add up the amounts together.

Find the figure for your total investment (this is referred to as cost basis for the purposes of tax.

Add in the brokers commission and all other fees used up to buy and sell stock to the total stock price.

Multiply the selling price for each share with the total number of shares you sold to get your total earnings from the sale.

To get the profit, deduct the total cost basis from the sum total of the earnings.

If you get a cost basis that is higher than the earnings from your sale then you will get a negative number meaning that you experienced a loss for that investment. A positive number on the other hand means a profit.

You should always separate different stock transactions based on the length of time you've held that penny stock. This is because the profit for an investment that is held for more than a year can qualify for much less long term capital gains tax rates whereas short term profits (those that are owned for less than an year) don't.

Lastly, we will discuss how to keep your costs and probability of losses low.

Limiting Losses to Increase Profitability

As an investor, it is pretty much inevitable to come across losing stocks. But the level at which these will damage your portfolio depends on how you will handle them. Basically, there are 3 ways to do this:

Price Barriers

A price barrier is a level at which a share price has a hard time falling through e.g. a lower trend line or a support level. Identifying a barrier price can be done through personal research or professional investment research.

For instance, the shares of XYZ can sink up to 1 dollar level a couple of times but can always bounce back and never go below a dollar. This basically means that they may have a support level at a dollar.

Support levels exist due to the stronger buying pressures at the prices compared to the selling prices which ensures that the share price remains at or above the support. Once you identify the support level, go ahead and place your order to buy shares close to the support level but a bit above.

Assuming that you want to buy 2000 penny stocks of a company XYZ at $1.03 – the most effective way to go about it would be to closely monitor the penny stock until it hit a dollar and then begin moving higher to confirm that the support level has been held. After you've confirmed this, put an order to buy shares when they rise away from the dollar.

Stop Loss Orders

A stop loss order is an order to a broker to buy or sell a stock once it reaches a specific price. It is specially designed to limit your loss on a security position.

Just after you get your hands on your shares, put a stop loss order right away below the support level. If the shares rise in value, you continue holding them but when they move to or below the level of your stop loss order then the sell order is activated and your shares are sold at the price therein.

For instance, for our XYZ shares, you would place a stop loss for the 2000 shares at $0.98. If the share price falls below or to $0.98 then this is where your stop loss order kicks in and you end up selling the shares at a loss of approximately 4% plus commissions.

When the support level stays intact and the price of the penny stock maintains above a dollar, then you will have profitably purchased in very near the short term bottom in terms of price. Basically, you will be in a profit's position when the share price travels higher together with the extra insurance of the support level which is just under your position.

You should therefore, adjust your stop loss order upwards if the price of the penny stock happens to rise. For instance, if the price goes past $1.20, you should move your stop order loss to around $1.09 and when they rise past $1.4 then you should increase your stop order loss to $1.29. This strategy will help keep your profits assured. You will be taking advantage of the price rise and your penny stocks will get sold the first time only that the company XYZ's stock price drops.

Making good use of stop loss orders has guaranteed the trading profit of quite a number of penny stock portfolios despite simply winning about only 30% of trades. The reason behind this is that the 70% losing trades were really limited and the gains were allowed to ride hence they exceeded the minimal losses.

Setting up a stop loss price:

When setting up a stop loss price, volatility is something you should highly consider. You really don't want to 'stopped out'. This just means that when the price sinks to the level of your stop order and your shares are sold and then the prices rise right away after the sale into a much more profitable zone.

When you place the opening stop loss order below the support level, it means that you have lessened the possibility of being stopped out in the beginning. Nevertheless, placing your stops correctly gets really complicated when you follow a price that is rising. You will need to decide on your own stop levels based on the penny stocks volatility, your personal investment style and the momentum of the share price trend.

The methodologies here will be best applicable if you have invested about $1,500 or more for each penny stock to minimize the commission cost as a percentage of the total investment value.

If you apply all strategies mentioned in this book, investing in penny stocks will be a bliss for you.

CONCLUSION

We have come to the end of the book. Thank you for reading and congratulations for reading until the end.

I truly hope you found the book valuable and actionable enough to walk you through your penny stocks investment journey. Use the information you've learned here to get started while setting yourself up for success from the onset.

If you found the book valuable, can you recommend it to others? One way to do that is to post a review on Amazon.

Thank you and good luck!

CONCLUS) N